The Silk Flower Arranger's Companion

Colour, design and harmony
using silk and paper
parchment flowers and foliage

PAT REEVES

THE
APPLE
PRESS

A QUINTET BOOK

Published by The Apple Press
6 Blundell Street
London N7 9BH

ISBN 1-85076-582-0

This book was designed and produced by
Quintet Publishing Limited
6 Blundell Street
London N7 9BH

Creative Director: Richard Dewing
Designer: Ian Hunt
Project Editor: Diana Steedman
Editor: Deborah Taylor
Photographer: Jeremy Thomas

Typeset in Great Britain by
Central Southern Typesetters, Eastbourne
Manufactured in Singapore by
Eray Scan Pte Ltd
Printed in Singapore
by Star Standard Industries (Pte) Ltd

ACKNOWLEDGEMENTS

Many thanks to the following for their help in supplying
items for the projects: Smithers Oasis U.K. Ltd,
Washington, Tyne & Wear; James Naylor Ltd, Redditch,
Worcestershire.

CONTENTS

INTRODUCTION

Creating a beautiful flower arrangement is an extremely satisfying task and an opportunity to use one's artistic talents by taking time to work with wonderful materials to create a design which is a joy to behold and, by its display in the home, give great pleasure to others.

The available range of silk flowers and foliage is vast. There are varieties available from Europe, the Americas, Asia and the Far East. Each country produces its own exotic flora: orchids, lilies, frangipani, *Strelitzia, Spathiphyllum, Matthiola,* roses and carnations. They are made from a wide range of materials including silk, cotton, polyester, textured linens, specially treated paper, plastic and even banana and coconut fibre.

It is important, when buying the flowers, to get the best quality you can, even though better quality may mean a higher price. Better quality flowers will give you better results which will be more realistic and satisfying.

The advantages of silk flower arrangements are many. They do not need constant care, they are long-lasting, and offer a vast range of blooms and leaves to work with. Today, many people lead hectic lives with little time for buying and arranging fresh flowers. A silk flower arrangement is the perfect answer.

DESIGN AND COLOUR

The Basic Principles of Design

It is important to understand a few rules about design before you begin with your first silk flower arrangement. The basic principles of design are dominance, balance, proportion, scale, rhythm, contrast and harmony. Let us take them one by one.

Dominance Dominance is a feature which every design needs. It is an area of heightened interest in the design, such as colour, shape or shine. But it must not be too strong or it will hold your attention too long and prevent you from looking into the design itself. Of all the colours, bright yellow has the greatest luminosity and will immediately stand out in an arrangement. The inclusion of a gift, or even a very shiny leaf can also catch your attention in the same way and provide a focus to a design.

Balance Within an arrangement balance is both visual and actual. Good visual balance is achieved when the flowers and foliage are in perfect harmony and not grouped to one side. Avoid using bright colours on one side of the design only, as your eye will be taken to that side and not into the arrangement as a whole.

Actual balance means that the arrangement is stable and will not fall over or lean to one side. If you are not sure whether your design is balanced, pick it up when you are halfway through and balance it on the palm of your hand to judge whether you need more weight on either side.

Proportion Proportion is the correct relationship between the parts which make up a whole. The Egyptians were the first people to use proportion in design, which is evident as soon as you see their wall paintings and friezes. But it was the Greeks who developed the Golden Rule of proportion which is still true today and should be applied to setting the proportion of your design. This rule, in arrangement terms, is that the height of the arrangement should be the sum of the width of the flower arrangement. For example, if your container measures 2 cm (¾ in), the width of the flower arrangement within the container should be 3 cm (1¼ in). The height of the arrangement, being the sum of the container and the width of the flower arrangement, should measure 5 cm (2 in) to achieve proportion. The same Golden Rule applies to volume. If the container is 2 cm³ (¾ in³), the flower material would need to fill 3 cm³ (1¼ in³), giving a total volume of 5 cm³ (2 in³). Your arrangement is then in perfect proportion.

ABOVE *The arrangement looks as if it would fall over – and it probably would.*

ABOVE *Here, the flowers are balanced throughout.*

Scale This is the relationship of the flowers and foliage to each other, to the container and to the place in which the arrangement is to be placed.

Think of a posy sitting in the centre of a small table – it is the correct scale for the table. But place that posy in a large cathedral and it would be completely out of scale. In the cathedral you would need a very large arrangement of large flowers, while conversely this large arrangement would be totally out of place on the small table.

Rhythm Rhythm can be achieved by the repetition of lines and of colours within a design to produce a harmonious sequence alternating with light and shade. Rhythm in design can be likened to the gentle curves left on the beach as the waves ebb, or a field of corn waving in the wind. The use of contorted hazel and willow within a design can also give this sense of movement even though none in fact exists.

Contrast The Chinese believed that harmony in the Universe was achieved by Yin-yang and this is shown in all ancient Chinese art. Yin is female and represented by the dark, the moon, grasses and budded flowers. Yang is male, sturdy and strong, and represented by light, sun, evergreen trees and open flowers. Yin-yang represents contrast. Notice and use the different shapes, forms and colours within a design to achieve good contrast. Flowers, foliage, moss and pebbles together with a contrasting container can produce an exciting arrangement.

Harmony This is the unity of all the materials being used in an arrangement to achieve a pleasing whole.

Harmony takes account of all the elements – the compatibility of the flowers and foliage, whether they sit more happily in a vase than a container, and whether the arrangement blends with the furnishings and colours it is set in.

The Basic Principles of Colour

Although there are established rules for its use, colour is also a very personal matter so let your feeling for colour shine through. But do bear in mind the rules as they do offer guidance when working out colour schemes to capture a particular mood.

What is colour? Colour is light as without light there is no colour. Pull back the curtains, let in the light and immediately experience colour, brightness, warmth, coldness, or serenity. The mood of a summer's day can be evoked by the colours pink, mauve and blue while white daisies, blue cornflowers and red poppies can transport us to Provence or Tuscany in May. Bare twigs, daffodils and snowdrops immediately capture the feeling of spring, while an arrangement of bare branches, with larch cones and moss beneath, convey the cold wind of winter.

The colour wheel is the natural arrangement of twelve hues all of which come from the three primary colours: red, yellow and blue. The three secondary colours, orange, green and purple are made by mixing two adjacent primary colours. The sections remaining in the wheel are the tertiary colours, achieved by mixing two adjacent secondary colours.

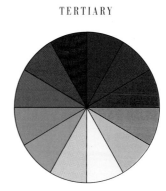

7

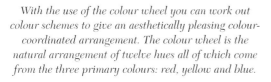

THE COLOUR WHEEL

PRIMARY   BINARY   TERTIARY

With the use of the colour wheel you can work out colour schemes to give an aesthetically pleasing colour-coordinated arrangement. The colour wheel is the natural arrangement of twelve hues all of which come from the three primary colours: red, yellow and blue.

The three secondary colours, orange, green and purple are made by mixing two adjacent primary colours. The sections remaining in the wheel are the tertiary colours, achieved by mixing two adjacent secondary colours.

By adding white to a colour you create a tint: white added to red makes pink; added to purple it makes lavender. However, the addition of black to a colour will darken it, to make a shade: red and black make crimson; and adding it to blue you make indigo. By adding grey (made by mixing white and black) you create a tone.

Monochromatic harmony. This is the simplest colour harmony. It is a combination of two or more tints, shades and tones of one primary colour. For example, pink, red, crimson.

Complementary harmony. This is a combination of two colours from the exact opposite sides of the wheel. For example, red and green, or blue and orange.

Split complementary. This is where one colour is used, not with its direct opposite, or complementary colour on the wheel, but with the opposite colour's two neighbouring colours. For example, purple, yellow-orange, yellow-green.

Near complementary. This is the relationship between one colour and one of the two colours that lie either side of its opposite colour. For example, red and yellow-green.

Triadic. This is when a harmony is made from three colours which are equidistant from each other around the wheel. For example, red, yellow and blue. When using this scheme remember to select one dominant colour using less of the second and even less of the third colour.

Tetradic. This is a four-colour harmony using colours which are equidistant from each other around the wheel. For example, red, yellow-orange, green, blue-purple. As with triadic harmony, one colour must be dominant and the others less so, the fourth colour being merely a touch.

Analogous. This harmony consists of three to four colours which are next to one another on the wheel but contain only one primary colour. For example, green, yellow-green, yellow and yellow-orange.

Achromatic. This means without colour but capable of reflecting light. For example, black, beige, grey and stone. These are the best colours to select for containers as they do not compete for attention with the colours in the arrangement.

Luminosity This is the quality that makes a colour stand out in poor light such as a dark corner that needs brightening. The most luminous colour is yellow but orange is also a strong colour with a feeling of warmth. Green has an air of safety that can balance the heat of a bright red and blue, a cool colour, conveys restfulness but does not excite the eye. Be careful when using blue that you use enough of it to make an impact, because too little will recede to nothing. Violet is the most receding colour, and should not be used in poor or subdued light while red is a positive and stimulating colour which is exciting and vibrant.

The choice of colour in your design is very important and it is necessary to know what mood it can produce. Consider the colours of the walls, the carpets and furniture of the room the design will be in. Look also at the style in which the room is decorated and then select flower material to enhance it. Consider the size of the room and the activities that go on in it. Give some thought too, to the people who use the room and how much walking about or sitting down they will do in it during a normal day.

PLACING ARRANGEMENTS IN THE HOME

The Kitchen

This is probably the busiest room in the house with people constantly on the move. The work tops will probably be in full use much of the time, but there is still sometimes space for an arrangement. The colours must match the scheme of the kitchen, but the arrangement can include not only silk flowers, but strings of artificial onions or garlic, fabric fruits and vegetables. All are very suitable for a busy kitchen with heat and steam invading the atmosphere. Fresh flowers would not last and dried flowers would become limp and drop.

The Downstairs Cloakroom

A posy of silk flowers can last indefinitely in this part of a house and will brighten this small room. The container needs to be carefully selected to blend with the fittings – coloured pottery or a ceramic pot to match tiles, or a glass vase if, perhaps, there are glass shelves, or maybe basketware to complement wood.

The Hall

This is the entry point for both guests and family. Put yourself in their place and take a critical look at your surroundings. Is there a bend in the stairs where an arrangement could stand? Remember that if your hall has a lot of traffic, wherever you place your flowers they need to be positioned where they will not be knocked over. Also if they are to stand on the floor, the container must be solid and heavy so they do not fall over. A low arrangement, on the other hand, is ideally suited to a hall table where it can be viewed to its best advantage, from above.

8

The Lounge

This is usually a restful area where people will sit rather than always being on the move. However, there may be occasions when visitors will be standing up or wandering around so the positioning of the arrangement is important.

An open fireplace can, during the summer months, become the focal point of a room, especially when it is filled with a large arrangement of summer flowers and foliage. But to be really effective, the flowers must match not only the container, but also the style of the room.

The Dining Room

Here, the flowers are often placed on the sideboard or in the middle of the dining table. Take a look at the decor and assess whether it is modern or traditional. Is the table made of glass or wood? Take into account the style and colour of the carpet and curtains. All these considerations will help you to decide on the design of your arrangement.

The arrangement for the sideboard can be quite substantial, as long as it is in proportion to the room. A front-facing asymmetrical design always suits this situation and, when linked in colour and materials to the table centre arrangement, can produce a stunning effect. A very long table need not have one main arrangement but could have several small posies placed at regular intervals down the centre.

When having dinner, people usually prefer to sit both sides of the table and talk across it, so they need to be able to see one another over the flowers or, if the arrangement is sufficiently high, to see each other beneath. This means you need to design a long and low arrangement or, alternatively, one on a stand which is above eye level (approximately 55 cm [22 in]). If you use a tall stand you must make sure it is stable enough to carry the arrangement safely.

Silk flowers and foliage are particularly suitable for the table as they do not drop petals or pollen, or attract unwanted insects to the table during a meal.

Bedrooms

The usual place for an arrangement in a bedroom is on the dressing table, which almost certainly will have a mirror, which means that the flowers will be viewed from all sides.

The Bathroom

A room which alternates between warm air and steam and where a dry atmosphere is not suitable for dried flowers. But silk flowers do provide the perfect answer, as they are long lasting under these conditions.

Analyse the bathroom for colour and for the mixture of textures. Ceramic tiles, plastics, laminated screens, and carpets will dictate the container for your arrangement. Select one to match one texture in the room, then think of which flowers you want to use. Perhaps lilies, irises, orchids or waxy tulips. The bathroom is a very functional room so keep the design small but complementary.

9

A GLOSSARY OF MATERIALS AND TECHNIQUES

Baskets Must complement both the furnishings of the room into which the arrangements will be placed, and the flowers and foliage they will contain. Whereas natural, rustic baskets would look out of place in a modern room they will be suitable to a room decorated in the cottage style.

When choosing a basket for a bridesmaid, remember how tall the girl is. The size of the basket must not only be in keeping with her height and weight but the fabric of the basket must also complement her dress and the flowers it will contain. You need to leave room between the top of the flowers and the handle to allow it to be carried comfortably. But the handle must not be so long that when it is held from the top and at arm's length it touches the ground.

Berries, fruits and vegetables Many of the designs in this book use berries, fruits and vegetables to make them more applicable to seasons or particular surroundings. They can be made of plastic, foam, wood or paper, and sometimes a combination of materials. When selecting them, think not only of size and colour but also of texture so that they blend into rather than dominate your design.

Should there be young children in the house, ensure these attractive items are glued firmly into position and that the arrangement is placed well out of their reach.

Bows The figure-of-eight is the most decorative and useful in the bow repertoire. When placed low in the centre of an arrangement it fills a space, masking not only the foam but the base of the stems.

Single figure-of-eight bow 1 Loop the ribbon in your left hand, pinching it between thumb and index finger, leaving one length twice the width of the ribbon.

2 With the other hand, make a second loop of ribbon the same length as the first and, without turning the ribbon over, pinch together on top of the first pinch. Keep holding the pinched ribbon.

3 Cut the tail at the top to the same length of the original tail. You now have the perfect figure-of-eight bow.

The two ribbon ends can be cut on a slant to give a neater finish. Place a 0.46 stub wire across the pinched centre of the bow and around the back. Twist off tightly. The tighter the wire, the more erect the loops of the bow will stand. A hook can be made in the other end of the wire with which to push it well down into the foam.

Double figure-of-eight bow with long tails Proceed as for the single figure-of-eight bow but before cutting the ribbon, make a second loop over the first loop, again pinching it together in the centre. Cut the last tail the same length as the first one. You then have two loops and two tails each side of the bow. To attach long tails of ribbon, cut a length twice the desired length. Take the long piece of ribbon and place it behind the bow you have already made, making the tails trail at different lengths. Place a 0.56 stub wire across and behind the pinched centre of the bow and twist firmly together.

Bun moss Natural clumps of moss gathered from woodlands and allowed to dry out. It is advisable to remove some of the backing to allow the moss to sit flatter on the foam.

Candles Add colour and interest to an arrangement. Remember, when using candles to position them safely away from the flowers in the design. If you do not want the candles to be lit, it is safer to cut the protruding wick to prevent accidents.

Cones Rather than buy these, collect them for yourself on a country walk. The variety used in the Christmas arrangements on pages 68–80 were especially selected for their size.

To support a cone, take a 0.46 stub wire and run it around the last row of the cone, working it down into the cone so that the wire does not show. Twist the two ends firmly together to prevent the cone slipping out.

Containers There are many types of containers that can be used in flower-arranging. I have chosen those I have in my own home: silver candelabra, goblets, kitchen scales, bronze loaf tins, jugs, etc. Look about your home to see what you have already selected to match your furnishings. Your friends will compliment you on your originality and it will have cost you nothing. You need only then select complementary flowers and foliage.

Ipma containers These are shallow plastic containers which are very reasonably priced and are available in various colours and shapes.

Oasis pop bowl A shallow, circular plastic bowl, particularly effective for posy-style arrangements.

Square-based O bowl A plastic container with a square base, but deeper than the pop bowl. More foam can be used in this container to hold a larger amount of flower material.

Tempo bowls A practical and decorative bowl made of glazed ceramic or terracotta, filled with foam, available in a variety of sizes.

10

Contorted hazel and willow These contorted varieties give height and interest with their intricate, graceful curves and angles. When inserting them into foam, a dab of glue will secure the lighter pieces. Heavier pieces need more support. For these, make a small hole in the foam with the end of the twig and fill the hole with glue. Push the twig well down into the hole you have made, then hold in position for a minute to allow the glue to harden.

Dew-drop roses A technique which makes the rose and its leaves appear to have been sprinkled with dew, creating an early-morning freshness to any arrangement in which they are included.

Dry image A range of silk flowers and foliage that have been treated to give a more realistic effect when used alongside natural materials such as twigs, cones, oyster fungus or moss.

Finland moss A natural lichen that has been treated with glycerine to make it soft and pliable. It does not dry out or shrink.

Foam Oasis sec dry foam is available in a wide range of shapes, in colours

green and brown. It allows many design possibilities. The foam has an outstanding grip for all types of designs and is easy to both cut and glue. It is fire retarded to German B2 Standard and is CFC-free. It can be obtained in bricks of 23 x 11 cm (9 x 4½ in), in cylinders 5 x 8 cm (2 x 3 in) in diameter and in cones of 9 cm (3½ in) base and 24 cm (9½ in) high, or 12 cm (4¾ in) base and 32 cm (12½ in) high. Oasis Sahara sec is a little less dense and more suited to lighter stems.

Oasis foam is available in an assortment of products many of which are featured in the variety of projects in this book.

Naylor posy pad A circular base of foam enclosed in its own container, giving a large surface on which to work. Available in two sizes, 33 cm (13 in), and 43 cm (17 in), these containers are ideal for table displays, as shown in the Table Spectacular (page 20).

Oasis igloo A cage specially designed to hold a small amount of foam together and not break up when inserting silk flower stems. These igloos can be glued on or into a container. They can be re-used since they easily pull off, leaving no mark behind.

Oasis mini deco Designed for creating miniature displays such as cake decorations, floral bottle displays and to decorate presents. Peel off the circle of backing paper, place the deco firmly on the surface you wish to decorate and create your miniature display. The icing remains edible when the decoration is removed.

Glue guns, pans and glue The Oasis low-melt glue gun is recommended because it has special advantages when used with silk materials. It operates at only 86°C and bonds quickly, in about 60 seconds, so there is no danger of you burning your fingers while holding materials in

place. Also, you do not have to wait long for it to dry.

The Oasis glue pan is another convenient tool and has the advantage of leaving both hands free, saving time and avoiding mess. The temperature can range from 76°C to 145°C (168°F to 293°F). Oasis glue pellets are recommended for high quality bonding. Having both hands free means that you can dip the end of a stem into the pan, shake off the excess and insert the wire stem firmly into place.

Glue sticks, used with the glue gun, take about 2–5 minutes to melt, while the glue pellets take about 10 minutes to dissolve. Both the glue gun and the glue pan can be left on while you work. Excess glue can be left to harden, ready for use next time. Low-melt glue does not damage surfaces and peels off when no longer required.

11

Hair pins These are used to anchor in place Finland moss, bun moss and other items. You can purchase German pins in different lengths, 10/25, 10/40 and 10/60, but it is so easy to make your own.

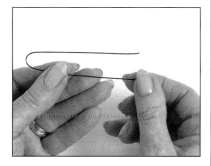

To secure Finland moss, take 0.71 stub wire and cut it in half. Take one half, bend it in half. Cut each end on the slant to give a better point to the pin.

For securing larger pieces of bun moss, use a 0.90 stub wire. Sometimes you will need a long pin, so just bend the 0.90 stub wire in half and cut the ends on the slant. For smaller pieces, the 0.90 wire can be cut in half and two pins made from one piece of wire. Always make your pins long enough to go through the material you are anchoring and well down into the foam.

Knives You will need one long knife to cut your foam to size. It is more economical to buy foam by the brick and cut it to the size and shape you require than to buy smaller individual pieces. Save any irregularly-shaped or small pieces as these can be used to pack the inside of a container and to fill any gaps. A small florist's knife is useful to chamfer (scrape or cut away) the edges of the foam, to produce a sloping side which is easier to use when creating your design.

Loomey stands These are tall pillars of clear plastic which are very light in weight and have a small circular platform on the top. They enable you to arrange flowers at different levels to create a stunning impact.

Mixed flower bunches As well as buying single stems of flowers or foliage, it is possible to purchase attractive mixed bunches of silk flowers which are bonded together into a posy. You can see how these have been used if you turn to the designs in the wedding section on pages 38–50. Take the bunches of flowers apart by cutting and rearranging them into your own design.

Mounting This is the procedure of attaching a wire to a stem to give it either extra length or stability.

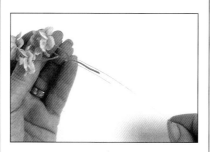

1 Select the weight and length of stub wire you require. Bend one end of the wire so it folds back about 2 cm (3/4 in) to make a hair pin. This is laid alongside the stem.

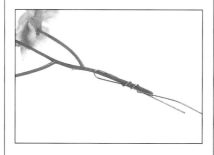

2 Either tape the wire and stem firmly together, or twist the ends around the short end for two or three turns and then pull down to straighten.

Oyster fungus This is a natural tree fungus which has been treated and dried to keep its shape. Anchor it to the foam by either glueing it into place or by inserting it into the foam. Large pieces will need to be support-wired.

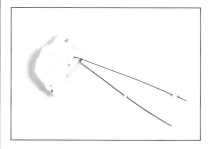

1 Take a 0.90 stub wire and cut one end on the slant. Carefully push the cut end through the fungus until 4–5 cm (1½–2 in) of wire protrudes.

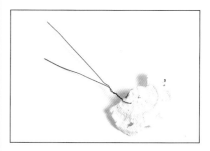

2 Bend the protruding wire back alongside the straight wire and twist up close to the fungus. Insert the wire and the end of the fungus against the foam so that the fungus sticks out at right angles.

Ribbons There are so many beautiful ribbons available today that it may be difficult to choose the best one. However, if you follow a few rules you will select the perfect ribbon for your arrangement.

The colour of the ribbon should tone with the flowers you are using. The width should be in proportion to the size of the flowers: if it is too wide it will dominate, and if too small it will be insignificant. Texture – never use a shiny ribbon with natural-looking materials, try hessian or web. Ribbon with a rough texture will echo moss, bark, wood and dry image flowers. Beautiful wedding gowns and wonderful flowers deserve high quality silk or satin ribbons. The ribbons sold in flower shops have been treated to stay crisp and bright and will hold their shape, unlike lingerie or dress ribbons.

Pleated ribbon To edge a container or basket with ribbon you will need 5 cm (2 in) wide ribbon. The best method is box-pleating which bends around a circular container and lies comfortably on the edge.

Make the pleats as shown, making sure the top edge remains straight. Staple the pleats in place but do not staple over a treble fold as you will have a rigid edge which will not bend around curves. When the two ends meet, ensure you finish with a complete pleat. Glue into place.

Scissors Stainless steel scissors are the best. They are very comfortable to hold and maintain their sharpness. I like to keep two pairs, reserving one purely for cutting ribbons.

Silk flower cleaner Oasis silk flower cleaner dry-cleans silk and fabric flowers and ribbons. You will be amazed at the difference a gentle shake or dust over with a very soft brush and a respray with silk flower cleaner can make. Give your finished arrangement a gentle mist of silk cleaner to help keep it clean and crisp. Some silk flowers can be washed in warm soapy water, although this is difficult to do

once they are part of a complete arrangement.

Stapler and staples These are required to secure pleats in ribbons to surround a container. The light, hand-held variety to take small staples is best.

Straw ring Rings of straw, willow, tree roots and tree bark are among the many types of ring available. When selecting a natural material remember that it is easy to get carried away with the appearance of the ring, but if you are going to cover it with silk flowers and foliage a plainer one may be more suitable. Also, bear in mind the weight. A Christmas door garland has to be hung, so think about how heavy it will be once it is finished and whether it will sit flat against the door. Straw is the perfect answer in this instance.

Tapes Pot tape or anchor tape is available in green or white and is used to secure foam to a container. Usually it is sufficient to place a dab of glue into the container before pressing in the foam to secure it. However, when you use heavier pieces of material, such as wood or long-stemmed flowers, it is safer to tape the foam into place.

Stem tape is available in two widths: for binding the stem of a flower which may need strengthening, or for lengthening when it is twined round a wire. It is slightly adhesive and so quickly binds to the stem and does not unravel easily.

Table decos These are produced by Oasis. They are oblong containers filled with foam and specially designed for arrangements where space may be at a premium or for table arrangements which need to be long and slim, as in the Christmas' table centre shown on page 69.

Wedding belles The Oasis wedding belle is a bouquet holder containing foam into which flowers can be arranged very easily. It has a delicate unobtrusive handle which combines attractive appearance with strength and suitability. The cage over the foam offers security yet leaves it easily accessible for the insertion of the silk flower stems. You will see how easy and quickly you can construct a beautiful wedding posy on page 46.

Wire There are many gauges of florist's stub wire, from the very finest to quite heavy. A good rule of thumb when deciding on the correct weight to use, is to twist the wire around the bottom inch of the stem to see if it will hold it up; if it flops over, you need a heavier gauge.

0.24 mm – a very fine wire, for stems of *Gypsophila* for example.

0.32 mm – for slightly heavier stems, such as lily of the valley, polyanthus or seventh heaven.

0.46 mm – for use with small bows of 1cm (½ in) ribbon, mounting Bere grass, Christmas roses, Poinsettia and attaching fir cones.

0.56 mm – for use with bows of 5cm (2 in) ribbon, especially where long tails of ribbon are to be attached.

0.71 mm – for twisting around cinnamon sticks; making hair pins to attach Finland moss.

0.90 mm – for mounting heavier stems such as chrysanthemums; attaching strings of onions, oyster fungus; making hair pins for candles and heavier bun moss.

1.00 mm – a heavy, strong wire for use with wood; for making circular stands on which to glue presents that need anchoring.

Wire cutters A good pair of wire cutters are needed to cut stems and to split silk flowers which are sold in bunches.

CHAPTER ONE

ARRANGEMENTS FOR THE TRADITIONAL HOME

STUNNING SILVER AND FLOWERS

Nothing graces a table better than flowers and candles. The soft mauves and whites of this arrangement blend beautifully with the silver candelabra.

YOU WILL NEED

Oasis igloos

Silver candelabra

Tall white candle

Delphiniums

Freesias

Scindapsis leaves

Blue-berry trail

Trail of ivy

Dry-image anemones

Scissors

Wire cutters

Low-melt glue gun and glue

1 Place the candle in the centre of the candelabra. Glue in the Oasis igloos on the other two candle holders. Remember that low-melt glue peels off easily and will not damage your candelabra. Add a small circle of leaves around the bases of the igloos.

2 Place in the centre of the igloo a stem of delphinium to simulate a candle. Make sure that the delphinium is straight and in line with the candle.

15

3 Surround the edge of the cage of the igloo with more scindapsis leaves and two trails of ivy, each one falling away from the centre and the candle. Place small pieces of the delphinium and their budded stems around the edge following the shape of the leaves.

4 Take one long trail of ivy and place it on the left-hand arrangement so that it falls across the face of the right-hand arrangement thereby linking the two arrangements. Complete the design by placing the freesias, the blue berries and the white dry-image anemones within the shape of the arrangement.

RIGHT *This elegant design with its symmetry and soft colours makes a beautiful table centre.*

DRESSING TABLE ARRANGEMENT

The dressing table in a guest bedroom is an ideal place for silk flowers. This arrangement has been designed to be set in front of a mirror so that it can be viewed from all sides.

YOU WILL NEED

White Oasis tempo bowl	Berry pick
Oasis Sahara foam	Green flower dream ribbon
White freesia	Scissors
Lily of the valley	Wire cutters
Mixed foliage	Low-melt glue and glue pan

1 Shape the foam to sit comfortably in the bowl and glue in firmly. Place the leaves of the lily of the valley around the lip of the bowl. Place the foliage 1.5 cm (½ in) from the rim to enable it to drape over the edge. Add another layer of leaves to give contrast.

2 Establish height with lily of the valley in the centre and smaller pieces around the edge. Add three placements of freesia around the lily of the valley and then fill in with more lily of the valley. Making sure none of the flowers protrude over the outer rim of leaves.

RIGHT Use a figure-of-eight bow on one side of the arrangement and balance it with some berries to complete the design.

18

SPECTACULAR
IN WHITE AND GREEN

A table arrangement for that very special occasion. Something that will make all your guests comment and impress them with your skills.

YOU WILL NEED

Naylor posy pad

Loomey stands

Oasis sec foam

Calathea leaves

Ivy leaves

Berry picks

Hellebore

Freesias

Lily of the valley

Bere grass

Finland moss

Low-melt glue and glue gun

Knife

Scissors

1 Chamfer off the outer edge of the foam to give it a smooth rise. Place the calathea leaves in two groups around the edge of the Naylor posy pad. Then, using ivy leaves, complete the circle. Glue small pieces of foam onto the top of the loomey stands and glue the stands firmly to the posy pad, pressing them down into the foam. Onto the foam on the top of the loomey stands glue on Finland moss to roughly cover them and into this place the bere grass and some of the leaves.

2 Complete the designs on the top of the loomey stands by adding bere grass and lily of the valley in a small posy design. Arrange the freesia, hellebore and berries so that they cover the foam. Complete the design by filling in any gaps with the Finland moss.

RIGHT *Check the design carefully for gaps as, being a table centre, it will be viewed from all angles. Fill in any remaining gaps with Finland moss to complete this impressive arrangement.*

ASYMMETRICAL ARRANGEMENT

The most important part of this arrangement is the design. An asymmetrical arrangement should have the basic shape of the letter L with one-third of the width on one side and two-thirds on the other. In technical terms, the height should be equal to the sum of the width. The depth of colour and shape of the flowers used on the left-hand side balance the arrangement. As this arrangement is to be placed high the flowers and foliages should gracefully fall down over the front.

YOU WILL NEED

Ipma container

Oasis sec foam

Antirrhinum

Roses

Delphinium

Seventh heaven

Calathea leaves

Coleus leaves

Eucalyptus

Trailing green foliage

Finland moss

Scissors

Wire cutters

Low-melt glue gun and glue

Oasis pot tape

1 Cut a block of foam 13 cm (5 in) high. Glue in and, if necessary, tape the foam to the container. Firmly insert the antirrhinum to one side and through the top, of the foam. Place a long piece of trailing foliage on the right and calathea leaves on the left-hand side of the design.

2 Add two more stems of antirrhinum following the line of the first one and add more foliage to mask the foam. Bear in mind that this arrangement has been designed to be placed high up, so some of the foliage must fall down over the front.

3 Insert the roses following the L-shape. Place seventh heaven on either side of the centre flowers. Using the remaining flowers, foliage and Finland moss to fill in any uncovered foam either by gluing or by anchoring with wire hair pins.

RIGHT *The success of this asymmetrical design relies on getting the proportions right between height and width.*

22

WEIGHING THE BALANCE

A very easy and quick-to-make design using the kitchen scales to
add interest in the kitchen. Fresh flowers are not always suitable
in the kitchen because of the heat and steam, but silk flowers, fruits and
vegetables are. Begin by arranging some vegetables in the scoop of the scales.

YOU WILL NEED

**Small terracotta bowl
containing Oasis sec foam**

Kitchen scales

Small string of onions

Assorted vegetables

Sweetcorn

Calathea leaves

Maple leaves

Queen Anne lace

Low-melt glue gun and glue

0.90 wire

Scissors

Wire cutters

1 Chamfer off the edges of foam within
the bowl and glue the bowl to the scales.

2 Drape the calathea and a few maple
leaves gracefully around the edge of
the foam.

RIGHT *Place a stem of the
maple leaves and the sweetcorn
in the centre of the foam as a
focal point. Take the string of
onions and mount on a 0.90
wire. Wrap the wire firmly
around the end of the stem and
make a small hook. Push the
hook firmly into the foam so
that the weight of the onions
will not pull the wire out of the
foam. Finish with small pieces
of foliage and the Queen Anne
lace to mask any visible foam.*

24

CHAPTER TWO

DESIGNS FOR THE MODERN HOME

MODERN HORIZONTAL DESIGN

A striking arrangement where the accent is on horizontal lines, and the central flowers are enclosed by crossed lines. A very modern arrangement designed for a low table.

YOU WILL NEED

Oasis pop bowl

Oasis sec foam

Plain candlestick or any other tall stand

Cinnamon sticks or any other straight sticks like bamboo

Ivy trails

Bere grass

Chrysanthemums

Orange seventh heaven

Oyster fungus

Maple leaves

Mushrooms

Scissors

Wire cutters

Low-melt glue gun and glue

1 Glue the bowl to the candlestick, then glue in the foam and chamfer the edges. Insert the cinnamon sticks on each side adding a little glue to the ends before pushing them in. They must be very firm to provide a platform for the other horizontal material. Put in the large leaves, the maple leaves and some oyster fungus around the base of the foam.

2 Place the ivy and the bere grass on top of the cinnamon sticks positioning them horizontally across the arrangement. Place bere grass on top of the oyster fungus both the front and back so it falls downwards over the edge. Insert the chrysanthemums, mushrooms and seventh heaven into the flat area of foam left on the top.

3 Finally, take the outer ends of the bere grass, coat the tips with glue and fold them over the centre of the design and down between the flowers and into the base of the foam to give the arrangement a caged effect.

4 Gently ease the flowers and the foliage to one side to enable you to insert the ends of the bere grass.

ABOVE *This unusual design is particularly suited to low positions. It relies on the strong horizontal structure given by the cinnamon sticks for its shape.*

GOING UP IN PARALLEL

In this arrangement, all the flowers and accessories are arranged in a vertical position following the natural way that the real flowers would grow. This is an ideal design for a corner of a room.

YOU WILL NEED

Oasis tempo bowl

Oasis sec foam

Stockade of small sticks

Delphinium

Thistle

Finland moss

0.71 stub wire hair pins

Scissors

Wire cutters

Low-melt glue gun and glue

28

1 Cut a piece of Oasis sec foam 7.5–10 cm (3–4 in) deep and glue it securely into the tempo bowl. Run a ring of low-melt glue around the outside of the top lip of the bowl and press the stockade of sticks around it, holding it for a few seconds so the glue has time to set.

2 Pin Finland moss onto the area of the foam exposed at the gateway of the stockade. Pins can be made by cutting in half a 0.71 wire and then folding the two pieces in half to make hair pins.

RIGHT *Make two placements of the delphinium, one of them a third taller than the other and leaving a clear pathway between them. Position the thistle vertically, low down in the front of the arrangement giving added interest to the gateway in the front of the design.*

M O D E R N   H O M E

ECONOMY WITH INTEREST

A design ideally suitable for that awkward corner or narrow shelf where space is at a premium. With this design it is imperative that the flowers selected enhance the colour and texture of the furnishings in the room.

YOU WILL NEED

Oasis tempo bowl

Oasis sec foam

Cinnamon sticks or any other straight twigs

Iris

Small green pumpkin

Queen Anne lace

Green fern

Begonia rex leaves

Low-melt glue pan, glue gun and glue

Scissors

Wire cutters

1 Place cinnamon sticks firmly into the foam, then take them out and fill the hole left with glue and then replace them holding them there for a few seconds until the glue hardens. Place the iris close to the cinnamon sticks, preferably within the curve of the stick.

2 Place the begonia rex leaves and the fern around the edge of the foam.

3 Dip the end of the pumpkin stick into the glue pan and place it well down into the surface of the foam. Add some more iris following the line of the cinnamon sticks.

RIGHT *Recess the Queen Anne lace right down into the surface of the foam to give balance to the small pumpkin and interest and texture to the base of the arrangement.*

VICTORIAN ROSES

Only these five stems of beautiful Victorian roses are needed
to give colour and movement to any dark corner of your home: the
bend in the stairs, the space under the stairs, or in any corner of the room
that has little natural light.

YOU WILL NEED

Tall glass container

**Hydrolecca pebbles to fill
the container**

Victorian roses

Caladium leaves

1 Fill three-quarters of a tall glass
container with the hydrolecca pebbles.

2 Put in the outer ring of caladium
leaves so that they form a collar to the
top of the container and then hold
them in place by adding a few more
pebbles.

RIGHT *Finally, add the rose stems so
that they form an attractive overall
shape which enhances, and is in
proportion to, the container. Fill the
rest of the vase with pebbles to keep
the whole arrangement secure.*

BLOCKED DESIGN WITH A DIFFERENCE

This arrangement is designed to be viewed from above and is ideal for a low table. It is very modern and a firm favourite in Europe.

YOU WILL NEED

Naylor posy pad

Coleus leaves

Strawberries

Roses

Azalea

Spray carnations

Delphinium

Bere grass

Dry statice and cereal heads

Low-melt glue gun and glue

Scissors

Wire cutters

0.46 stub wire

34

1 Chamfer off the edges of the foam to allow the leaves to fall gracefully down over the edge of the container.

2 Place coleus leaves around the edge of the posy pad to give a circular edge, then mount pieces of the bere grass on 0.46 wires and insert them at the outer edge of the posy pad above the coleus leaves.

3 Place each of the flower varieties in groups to cover the base. Do not scatter them separately across the foam. For the best effect, use different colours and textures next to each other. The strawberries make an excellent section in this design.

RIGHT Dip the ends of the bere grass in low-melt glue and arch them over the design and down into the foam to add extra interest.

TABLE CENTRE
OF FRUIT AND FABRIC

There are many excellent ready-made fruit and berry swags available and this arrangement uses one with the addition of bark strips and webb ribbon to create a centrepiece with a difference.

YOU WILL NEED

Fruit and berry swag	**Webb ribbon**
Bark strips	**Low-melt glue gun and glue**

1 Take the swag of fruits and berries and gently pull all the fruits and berries up into a more interesting design.

2 Soak the bark strips in warm water for 10 minutes. Then, when they are nearly dry, wind them through and over the fruits, gluing them down into the design. Hold them in place until the glue has set.

ABOVE *Finish this simply design by winding the ribbon through the swag and securing it with glue. The wood and the ribbon give the design more impact.*

CHAPTER THREE

THE WEDDING

BRIDESMAID'S BASKET

Dainty and colourful, a little basket of flowers to delight any little
bridesmaid. The flowers used echo those in the bride's bouquet on page 46,
giving a theme to the wedding flowers.

The flowers used echo those in the bride's bouquet on page 46,

YOU WILL NEED

Small basket

Oasis sec foam

Dew-drop rose

Dry-image roses

Dry-image scabious

Spray carnations

Bere grass

Green leaves

Eucalyptus

Chiffon ribbon

Moire ribbon

**Low-melt glue gun
and glue**

Scissors

Wire cutters

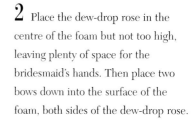

1 Wind the handle of the basket with
moire ribbon and secure it with a dab
of low-melt glue. Cut the Oasis sec
foam to a shape to fit in the base of the
basket and glue it in with low-melt
glue.

39

2 Place the dew-drop rose in the
centre of the foam but not too high,
leaving plenty of space for the
bridesmaid's hands. Then place two
bows down into the surface of the
foam, both sides of the dew-drop rose.

3 Place foliage around the edge of the foam to cover the base of the basket. Then insert pieces of bere grass above the foliage so that the ends fall over the edge of the basket.

4 Next, insert the spray carnations, the foliage and bere grass to make the outside ring of flowers.

5 Fill in the space left with dry-image roses, scabious and eucalyptus.

RIGHT *Finally, to finish off this pretty basket, use low-melt glue to attach a bow with long tails to the handles.*

WEDDING CORSAGE

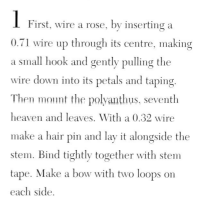

A graceful corsage of small flowers designed to grace the wedding outfits of the mothers of the bride and bridegroom. It is both light in weight and easy to make.

YOU WILL NEED

Dew-drop rose

Polyanthus

Seventh heaven

Rose leaves

Ivy leaves

Ribbon 2.5 cm (1 in) wide

Stem tape

0.32 stub wire

0.71 stub wire

Scissors

Wire cutters

42

1 First, wire a rose, by inserting a 0.71 wire up through its centre, making a small hook and gently pulling the wire down into its petals and taping. Then mount the polyanthus, seventh heaven and leaves. With a 0.32 wire make a hair pin and lay it alongside the stem. Bind tightly together with stem tape. Make a bow with two loops on each side.

2 Holding the flowers in one hand, build the corsage starting with an ivy leaf then seventh heaven, then another ivy leaf slightly lower down and to one side. Continue by adding the polyanthus flower and the central rose, holding them tightly in one hand. Gradually add other flowers and leaves to the design working down to form a natural stem.

3 Next, place the bow of ribbon in place on top of the stems. At this stage you can move the flowers by gently pulling them up or down.

RIGHT *Complete the design by adding the ivy leaves behind the bow and taping the stems together. Tease the corsage into a pretty shape and make sure the pin is covered when placed on the wedding outfit.*

TABLE CENTRE
FOR GUESTS' TABLES

This very pretty table centre, which echoes the bouquets of the bride and bridesmaids, will look graceful on any table for wedding guests. It also makes an excellent thank-you present for anyone who has helped make the wedding day special.

YOU WILL NEED

Oasis pop bowl

Oasis sec foam

Candle

Mixed-rose bunch

Seventh Heaven

Length of 5 cm (2 in) wide moire ribbon

Stapler and staples

Low-melt glue gun and glue

Scissors

Wire cutters

1 Box pleat enough ribbon to encircle the bowl. Run a little glue around the rim of the bowl and press the ribbon firmly into place. Glue the foam into the container and place a candle firmly into its centre.

2 Cut the flowers from the stem of the mixed-rose bunch using the remaining leaves to arrange around the edge of the foam but making sure that they do not hide all of the ribbon edge.

3 Fill in the centre of the design with the roses from the mixed bunch, keeping them low onto the surface of the foam.

RIGHT *Around the base of the candle add a few stems of seventh heaven to lift and lighten the design.*

BRIDAL BOUQUET TO CHERISH

A bride's posy-style bouquet of vibrant colours is perfect to grace that very special day. Surely she will not want to throw this bouquet to the guests, but would prefer to keep it as a memento of her wedding day.

YOU WILL NEED

Oasis sec wedding belle

Dew-drop roses

Dry-image roses

Spray carnations

Polyanthus

Bere grass

Grey rose leaves

Dry-image scabious

Chiffon ribbon

1 cm (1/2 in) satin ribbon

0.71 stub wire

Scissors

Wire cutters

Low-melt glue gun and glue

1 Insert five grey rose leaves around the edge of the wedding belle placing them well down on the cage of the holder. They can be tipped with glue before inserting for extra stability.

2 Insert a dew-drop rose in the centre of the foam and two more on either side of it. The ends of the roses can also be tipped with glue.

3 Insert bere grass over the edging leaves so that they fall gracefully over the edge of the foliage. Above the bere grass insert the spray carnations keeping to the circular posy shape and spacing them evenly.

RIGHT *Between the dew-drop roses and the spray carnations place a circle of dry-image roses and scabious. Make bows with the ribbon leaving long tails to fall down the front of the bride's dress. Insert the ribbons below the central rose.*

WEDDING
TOP-TABLE ARRANGEMENT

This arrangement is designed for the top table at the wedding reception.
It is placed towards the front edge so that the ribbons can fall down the
front of the table.

YOU WILL NEED

Oasis maxi table deco

Candles

Aralia leaves

Scindapsis leaves

Begonia rex leaves

Dew-drop roses

Spray carnations

Delphinium

Seventh heaven

Bere grass

Dry-image mixed rose bunch

Length of 5 cm (2 in) wide moire ribbon

Scissors

Wire cutters

Low-melt glue gun and glue

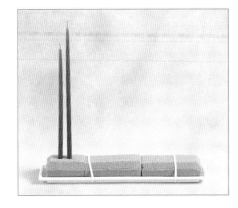

1 Place the candles firmly into the deco foam and at one end.

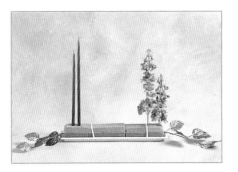

2 Place two stems of delphinium at the other end of the foam to establish the height of the design while leaving space in the centre. Place scindapsis leaves at each end of the design so that they flow out and away from the foam.

3 Fill in around the edge of the design with the rest of the foliage keeping varieties together to form interesting patterns.

4 Use the remainder of the flowers in groups to cover the foam but keeping them low to the surface of the foam.

ABOVE *The design is completed with a bow with beautiful trails to fall down the front of the top table.*

THE WEDDING

DECORATING TABLES

An economical and quick method of decorating wedding tables using
pretty posies and ribbons which echo the wedding colour-scheme.

Roses

Small carnations

Rose leaves

**Length of 5 cm (2 in) wide
moire ribbon**

Chiffon ribbon

Stapler and staples

**Low-melt glue gun
and glue**

Scissors

Wire cutters

Stem tape

50

1 Pleat the moire ribbon until you
have enough to make a circle, then
staple it together at the back of the
pleat. Make a figure-of-eight bow of
chiffon ribbon. Then, holding the rose
and spray carnations together in one
hand, circle them with leaves and tape
them together to make a posy.

RIGHT *Place the posy through
the centre of the circle of moire
ribbon and then touch the
backs of the leaves with low-
melt glue so that the ribbon is
held against the backs of the
leaves. Make as many posies as
you need to decorate the table
then pin them so they are
equally spaced around the rim
of the table. Link them
together with some moire
ribbon which can be pinned to
the table cloth.*

CHAPTER FOUR

FLOWERS FOR THAT SPECIAL OCCASION

Mother's Day Gift **52**

A Breath of Spring **54**

Flowers, Fruits and Foliage **56**

Silver Wedding Arrangement **59**

Sign of the Zodiac **62**

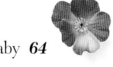

Gift for a New Baby **64**

Hospital Arrangement **66**

MOTHER'S DAY GIFT

Dry-image is the name given to a range of silk flowers, which have been treated to give them a natural look. This arrangement using dry-image flowers includes a gift of Christian Dior talcum powder. The flowers have been selected to match the packaging of the gift and enough flowers and leaves have been used to allow for a few of them to be repositioned after the gift has been removed to make a lasting arrangement.

YOU WILL NEED

Oasis white tempo bowl

Oasis sec foam

A gift

Green leaves

Trails of grey ivy

White dry-image scabious

White dry-image small roses

Grey rose leaves

Grey and gold bows

Natural Finland moss

1.00 stub wire

Oasis white pot tape

Scissors

Wire cutters

Low-melt glue and glue gun

1 Bend the wire into a ring to fit underneath the gift. Tape it to the base of the gift with tape. Chamfer the edges of the foam and glue it into the bowl. Place the gift in the centre of the foam so hiding the wire in the foam's surface. Arch the grey ivy over the gift like a basket handle.

2 Place large leaves around the edge of the container, the grey rose leaves first and then the green leaves to give contrast to the base of the design. Using the small roses place them at intervals around the edge of the design, then insert the scabious in the spaces left.

3 Complete the design with bows and moss, ensuring that all the foam is masked.

RIGHT By choosing flowers and leaves to make this arrangement complement the colours in your gift, you create two presents in one.

52

53

A BREATH OF SPRING

With the selection of a natural-bark basket, daffodils and iris which contrast
with the bare twigs, this arrangement brings a breath of spring into your home.
The little chicks in their baskets can be added for the Easter holiday period.

YOU WILL NEED

A natural basket	Bun moss
Oasis sec foam	Chicks in their nest
Iris	Scissors
Daffodils	Wire cutters
Contorted willow	Low-melt glue gun and glue sticks
Selection of green leaves	
Ferns	Tree bark
Ivy	

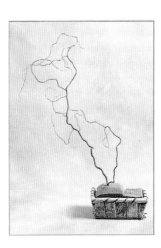  

1 Cut the foam 2.5 cm (1 in)
higher than the edge of the
basket and to fit the shape.
Then cut it away so it is level
with one side of the basket.
Touch the end of the contorted
willow with glue and place it in
the middle of the highest side
of the foam.

2 Place the iris in the centre
of the highest piece of foam
within the lines of the willow.

3 Use the bun moss to cover
the lower side of the foam.
Arrange the ivy and some of
the other leaves so that they
fall over the edge of the basket.
To the right of the willow,
arrange the ferns on the left
with the daffodils.

RIGHT *Decorate the arrangement
by gluing the chicks' nest in place
and scattering the surface with
pieces of tree bark.*

SILVER WEDDING ARRANGEMENT

Twenty-five years of marriage is a milestone which is usually marked with a party. A gift of something silver is usual and here the silver goblet is used as a container for the design. The dew-drop roses will glisten in the light and echo the silver container.

YOU WILL NEED

Silver goblet or silver container

Oasis sec foam

Dew-drop roses

White freesias

Seventh heaven spray

Azalea spray

Silver-grey ivy leaves

Bere grass

Silver ribbon

Scissors

Wire cutters

1 Cut and shape the foam so it sits well down in the container. Outline the symmetrical design by placing in the tallest azalea spray.

2 Place the long strap leaves of the freesia around the edge of the container, making sure that the height of the design is equal to the width.

60

3 Place the silver-grey ivy leaves and the bere grass around the base of the design to soften the strong lines of the azalea.

4 Insert the roses and some of the azalea through the centre of the foam. Make a bow from the silver ribbon and place it in the centre and well into the surface of the foam. Complete the design with the freesias and seventh heaven keeping within the triangular outline of the arrangement. Add small pieces of bere grass to soften the picture.

RIGHT *A dew-drop rose placed on the table under the arrangement completes a beautiful picture.*

SIGN OF THE ZODIAC

A birthday arrangement with a difference. This design uses the birth-sign's flowers and tree so that it has a special meaning. This design is for a Gemini where the special flower is lily of the valley and the tree is nut-bearing.

YOU WILL NEED

Ipma bowl	Zodiac ribbon
Oasis sec foam	Blue and gold parcel pick
Contorted hazel	Low-melt glue gun and glue
Selection of green leaves	Scissors
Hazelnuts	Wire cutters
Lily of the valley	

62

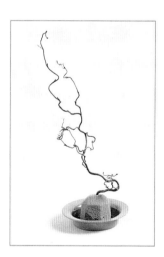

1 Cut and chamfer a piece of foam that is smaller than the base of the bowl and glue it into place. Make a small hole in the foam for the contorted hazel and fill it with glue. Push the contorted hazel into the hole and hold while it sets.

2 Insert the lily of the valley in a dainty clump at the base of the hazel, using some of the leaves to cover the foam.

3 Place a double-loop bow into one side of the arrangement, with the word Gemini showing to the front, and balance the other side of the arrangement with the blue parcel pick. Fill the space in the container with hazelnuts.

RIGHT Using the tree and flower related to someone's birth-sign makes a special birthday gift.

HOSPITAL ARRANGEMENT

Hospitals, by necessity, have to be warm and fresh flowers do not last long in this environment. Silk flowers are the perfect answer to this problem. Remember: if you want your arrangement to be placed on the patient's locker then it must be small and neat although it can have height.

YOU WILL NEED

Small Oasis tempo bowl

Tall stem of foliage

Selection of green leaves

Green berry pick

White freesia

Fir cones

Scissors

Wire cutters

Low-melt glue gun and glue

66

1 Arrange the dark green leaves around the edge of the foam with the lighter green leaves in between and at regular intervals to form a circular shape.

2 Place a tall stem of foliage in the centre of the foam to establish the height of the design. Remember to keep it in proportion to the base material.

RIGHT *Place the freesia around the central stem of foliage making sure that none of the flowers go beyond the outer circle of leaves. Complete the design by adding, low onto the foam, small leaves, the green berry pick and some fir cones to give texture and interest.*

CHAPTER FIVE

IDEAS FOR CHRISTMAS

CINNAMON AND CANDLES FOR CHRISTMAS

An enchanting centrepiece designed to grace the Christmas table, but low enough
not to obscure the person sitting opposite. It is also slim enough not to fill the
precious space at the centre of the table. The light and heat from the candles
will warm the cinnamon sticks to give a seasonal aroma to the room.

YOU WILL NEED

Oasis midi table deco	Pine cones	1 cm (½ in) wide tartan bows
Gold candles	Christmas picks	1.00 stub wire
Cinnamon sticks	Poinsettia	Wire cutters
Roses	Oyster fungus	Scissors
Holly	Finland moss	Low-melt glue and glue pan
Ivy	Pot tape	

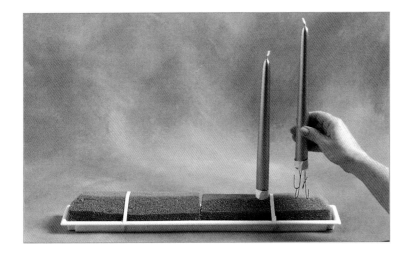

1 Chamfer off the edges of the table deco
foam. This removes the angular edge and
makes arranging easier. Place pot tape around
the Oasis midi table deco for extra support.
Using 1.00 wire make two prongs to raise the
candles away from the foam. Tape the prongs
to the candle with pot tape then place the
candles in position.

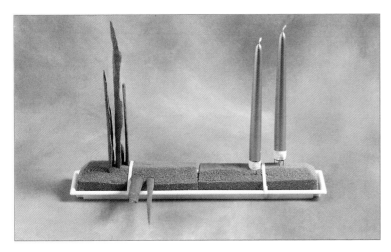

2 Push cinnamon sticks firmly into place at
the other end of the foam to balance the
height of the candles. Place two more
cinnamon sticks into the foam facing forward
horizontally to give extra interest to the
design.

3 Encircle the foam with holly and ivy in interesting groups, placing them a third of the way up from the lip of the container, flowing downwards to hide it. Glue in laterally, to echo the cinnamon sticks, the oyster fungus mounted on wire. Set one piece on each side.

4 Add the tartan bows between the edging foliage to add colour and texture to the base material.

RIGHT *Complete the design with Christmas picks, roses, poinsettia and pine cones. Fill in any gaps with Finland moss.*

CHRISTMAS DOOR-GARLAND

Natural holly can scratch the door of your home, as can the wire frames. This design is exciting and completely different and will not harm a beautiful wooden door. It is made on an interesting natural ring made of straw.

YOU WILL NEED

Straw ring

Ivy trails

Holly with berries

Finland moss

Small parcels

Length of 1 cm (1/2 inch) wide tartan ribbon

Length of 5 cm (2 in) wide wired tartan ribbon

Stapler and staples

Low-melt glue and glue gun

Wire cutters

Scissors

1 Make a loop with a length of 5 cm (2 in) tartan ribbon from which to hang the straw ring. Join the ribbon with enough staples to hold it firmly in place, bearing in mind the finished weight of the garland.

2 Pull the ribbon around until the staples are hidden at the back of the straw ring.

3 Twine the holly and ivy together to make a single piece long enough to cover the straw ring. Glue into place, holding each piece until it has set. Then glue on the little bows of tartan ribbon and the small parcels. Using Finland moss, cover any gaps.

RIGHT *Make a bow with the 5 cm (2 in) tartan ribbon leaving long trailing ends. Glue it to the bottom of the ring to complete the design.*

72

BOTTLE WITH A DIFFERENCE

A bottle of Champagne or bubble bath is made extra special by
decorating it with flowers.

YOU WILL NEED

Oasis mini-deco

Bottle

Small assorted foliage

Christmas roses

Bere grass

Gold bow with a wire

Finland moss

Low-melt glue and glue pan

Scissors

0.32 wire

1 Make sure the surface of the bottle is clean.
Peel off the backing strip of the mini-deco and
place it firmly against the bottle.

2 Insert small pieces of foliage around the edge
of the mini-deco, adding some bere grass around
the edge.

RIGHT *Dip the ends of the Christmas
roses in glue before positioning.
Dip bow's wire into glue and press
into the middle of the design.
Bend some of the bere grass into the
center of the design by dipping the
ends in glue. Mask any foam with
Finland moss.*

IDEAS FOR CHRISTMAS

DECORATED PARCEL

We all give a present at Christmas to someone who is very special to us. The present is usually special and chosen with love and care. Here is an easy way to decorate it to make it even more special.

YOU WILL NEED

A Christmas pick selected to match the wrapping paper

Gold ribbon to tie around the parcel

Bow with four loops each side

Finland moss

Low-melt glue and glue pan

Scissors

Wire cutters

76

1 Bind the parcel with the gold ribbon, lengthwise, sealing it with a dab of glue.

2 Make the gold bow remembering that you need four loops each side, and then stick this down onto the band of gold ribbon where the ribbon ends finish to hide the join.

3 Gently pull apart the Christmas pick cutting off the untidy ends. Glue the leaves from the pick into the centre of the bow, then stick down the gold berries, the decorative parcel and gold balls. To finish, dip a small piece of Finland moss in glue and place it well down in the design.

ABOVE *A present with that personal
touch to make it very special.*

FOLIAGE CHRISTMAS TREE

A tree with a difference, incorporating not just blue fir but evergreens like ivy and holly to give a contrast of colours and texture.

YOU WILL NEED

Oasis sec 60 cm (24 in) cone

Terracotta pot

Small branch for the trunk of the tree

Blue fir

Green leaves

Ivy and holly

Small parcels

Tartan bows

Fruits

Robins

Tree bark

Low-melt glue and glue gun

Scissors

Wire cutters

0.46 stub wire

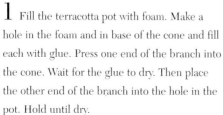

1 Fill the terracotta pot with foam. Make a hole in the foam and in base of the cone and fill each with glue. Press one end of the branch into the cone. Wait for the glue to dry. Then place the other end of the branch into the hole in the pot. Hold until dry.

2 To add foliage to the tree, begin at the base by inserting the blue fir in at an angle to give the tree a natural look. As you continue up the cone of the tree, add the holly and the ivy and the other leaves, working your way up in a circular fashion.

3 Take great care when you get to the top of the cone that you only use small pieces so as not to damage the foam. Do not pack the cone too tightly but leave space for the rest of the decorations.

4 Decorate the tree by glueing on the nuts, robins, small parcels and bows.

NEXT PAGE *A Christmas tree that will not drop its needles and will last for ever.*

IDEAS FOR CHRISTMAS